How To Regulate Your Lever Harp

Book One: The Loveland Lever

Steve Moss

Northside Press

Contents

Preface   1

1. What is Regulation?   5

2. Knowing Your Harp   11

3. The Loveland Lever   17

4. Tools Needed   25

5. Setup   32

6. Noise Control   41

7. Intonation   49

8. Conclusion   57

9. Appendices   59

Acknowledgments   79

About the Author   81

Preface

The world of harps and harpers is a wonderful one, but it is a small one as well. Just as you can rarely walk into the average music store and walk out with a harp, it can be difficult to find professional maintenance and repair services. Many local music stores that offer repairs will refuse to work on harps due to a lack of knowledge, skills, and tools. This is understandable. Since there are relatively few harps in any given area, most stores will never see enough harps to justify the time and expense of learning to repair and service them.

Professional harp technicians like myself travel the world servicing harps, but we are a small number covering a large area. A professional technician may only visit your area once a year or less. If you live far from a metropolitan area, you may need to drive for hours to meet a technician.

Harp makers can often service harps, though some will only work on those they made. If you are lucky enough to live near someone who is happy to service your harp, you will probably do just fine without this book. But then again, you may wish to buy it just to better understand how your instrument works.

Even if you have your harp serviced by a maker or traveling technician, emergencies can arise. They have a funny tendency to do so just when you're about to go onstage or play for a wedding. Having the knowledge and tools to fix regulation problems can help you get yourself out of a tight spot when there's no time to call a technician.

Should every harper regulate their own harp? Certainly not. It takes time and practice to learn. It also requires an investment in tools. You may prefer to spend your time playing your harp instead. There's nothing wrong with that. On behalf of other professional technicians, I'll say we're happy to have your business. But if you're having trouble getting your harp serviced in your area, or if you'd like to know the basics of harp regulation in case of an emergency, even if you'd just like to know more about how your harp works, then this book is for you.

If you play the harp, you likely understand enough about the fundamentals of music to regulate harps. But you don't have to be a harpist to learn to regulate harps. You might be the spouse, significant other, or parent of a harpist, or a staff member at a music store who would like to do harp regulations. It is not necessary to be a harpist to regulate harps. However, you do need some basic knowledge about music in order to understand what regulation is and how it's done. In the instructions that follow, I will assume that you have a grasp of the basic elements of music theory and notation outlined in the list below. If you are not familiar with the terms used here, refer to Appendix A for a basic introduction to music.

1. You will need to be able to tune a harp using an electronic tuner. If you are a non-harpist or a beginning harpist, take some time to learn to tune well before trying to learn regulation.

2. You will need a basic understanding of music notation and key signatures, especially those of common major keys harps are tuned to, including C, F, B♭, and E♭.

3. You need to understand the difference between a diatonic pitch change (i.e. C to D) and a chromatic pitch change (i.e. C♮ to C♯). For more on this, see Appendix A.

4. You need to know what a half step is in music, and how the accidental symbols (♮, ♭ and ♯) affect a given pitch.

Understanding the basics of regulation and lever adjustments gives you greater control over your instrument's performance. Knowing how the mechanical parts work and what to do if something goes wrong can mean the difference between solving the problem or waiting months for someone knowledgeable to visit your city and take care of it for you. Even if, after reading this book, you decide to leave this work to someone else, I believe that understanding the process is invaluable in terms of your enjoyment and appreciation of your harp.

This book refers specifically to regulation of harps with Loveland levers, produced by the Loveland Harp Company and used on many different makes of harp.

If you are not sure what kind of levers your harp has, ask your teacher, the harp's maker, or compare them with the photos shown in Chapter 3 of this book.

Chapter One

What is Regulation?

Regulation Defined

I n a nutshell, regulation is a periodic maintenance procedure performed on both the lever and pedal harp. Its goal is to help the harp sound its best both by ensuring that it sounds in tune in any key, and by eliminating unwanted buzzing, sympathetic vibrations, or ticks and clicks caused by worn or loose mechanical parts. In the simplest terms, regulating a harp means adjusting it to sound its best.

In practice, regulation involves tightening loose screws, making slight position adjustments to levers, and tracking down and eliminating unwanted noise.

In its oldest, most traditional form, the harp did not have mechanical parts, such as levers or a pedal mechanism. Each string could be tuned to one note at a time, and the number of different pitches available to the player was limited by the number of strings. Modern harps are more complex, with the addition of ei-

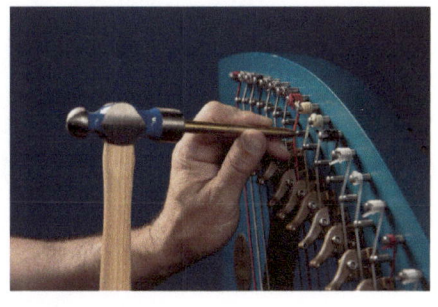

ther levers or a pedal mechanism to give the player access to a wider range of pitches without increasing the number of strings. In the case of the lever harp, which is the subject of this series of books, some or all of the harp's strings are equipped with what is known as a "sharping lever", or simply as a "lever". The lever is positioned so that when it is engaged, it shortens the length of the string, raising the string's pitch by one half step. This gives the player the ability to switch to a different musical key without retuning the strings.

Why does a harp need regulation?

When your harp was first made, the maker regulated it before selling and shipping it. Why then would you need to do it again from time to time? There are two main reasons. One is the natural changes that occur in a harp over time, which can alter the relationship between the strings and the position of their corresponding levers. Over time, under constant string tension, the harp's shape alters subtly but significantly. The neck and pillar are twisted and pulled slightly down toward the soundboard, and the soundboard is pulled slightly toward the neck. These gradual changes mean a lever that was adjusted for optimal position when the harp was new may need to be readjusted in order to keep the sharped pitch in tune. In the case of the Loveland lever, as we'll see, the bridge pin must also be adjusted in order to optimize intonation.

Figure 1-1. Sharping levers, when engaged, raise a string's pitch by one half step.

Another reason for regulation is wear and tear. As we move our harps around and play them, and as the seasons change year after year, small problems can arise. A screw holding a lever in place may become loose. The lever may twist slightly, placing it out of alignment with the string. A cam can become loose as well, resulting in a lever that won't stay engaged, or a muffled tone when the string is played.

How often should a harp be regulated?

Frequency of regulation for an individual harp depends on several factors: the amount the instrument is played, the environment where it is kept, the amount it is moved, and the sensitivity of the player's ear. Let's explore each of these in more detail.

The more a harp is played, the more it is tuned. This means it is always kept at tension, and the changes to the neck and soundboard that we discussed in the previous section will continue to happen over time. A harp that is never played is often not kept in tune. Over time, the strings gradually slacken, reducing the string pressure against the neck and soundboard. This slows the process of time-related changes somewhat. A harp that is never played, therefore, may not need regulation as often as one that is. This is not to say that one shouldn't tune too often. Quite the contrary. A harp that is not kept in tune will not stay in tune when you do want to play it. Just remember that regular use demands a regular schedule of maintenance.

With a few exceptions, harps are made of wood, which is susceptible to seasonal changes in humidity. In humid weather, wood absorbs moisture from the air by osmosis, causing it to swell. In drier weather, the moisture returns to the air by the same process, resulting in shrinkage. Over time, this cyclical process can result in slight position changes of the levers and bridge pins, which can result in regulation issues.

Moving a harp frequently can cause slight changes in lever or bridge pin position. Rough handling can cause levers to be bent or broken as well. Moving a harp to different micro-climates, such as from home to recital hall or teaching studio, can cause minor changes due to humidity and moisture, and all of these factors together can contribute to a need for the harp to be regulated.

Finally, some harpists' ears are more sensitive to intonation than others. The longer one plays music, the more discerning one's ears can become. A harp that sounds fine to a beginner may sound slightly sour and in need of regulation to a more experienced professional.

Since there are so many variables in each of these factors, there is no universal rule on how often a harp will need service. That said, I generally recommend to my customers that lever harps be regulated every five years, or more often if the harpist hears troublesome noises or finds that the harp has difficulty staying in tune after switching keys. While a lightly played, seldom moved instrument may not exhibit problems after five years, it is still not uncommon by that point for lever screws to become slightly loose or bridge pins to change position. Minor intonation issues that are not yet noticeable can be corrected before they become serious enough for the harpist to detect. Thus, a five-year regulation schedule prevents problems before they become a distraction for the majority of harpists.

Why regulate your own harp?

The primary advantage to regulating your own harp, as I mentioned in the Preface, is the limited availability of professional technicians. Unless you happen to live in the same city as a technician or harp maker, you may only have a technician visit your area once or twice a year. If you live far from an urban area, a technician may never come within 100 miles of you. If you can do your own regulation, you will not be dependent on someone else's travel schedule or forced to drive several hours for a regulation. You may still decide to have your harp professionally regulated every few years, but in the meantime you will have the knowledge of how to troubleshoot and fix problems that arise when no technician is available.

As with any kind of maintenance, it costs less to regulate your own harp than to pay someone else to do it, so that can be an advantage as well, especially if you have more than one harp to maintain.

Do-it-yourself harp regulations are not for everyone, though. They take patience and a tolerance for tedium. You'll need some specialized tools and a willingness to be kind to yourself if you make a mistake you can't fix alone.

Disclaimer

While I encourage you to consider learning to maintain your own instrument, I must also emphasize that you do so at your own risk. The author and publisher of this book take no responsibility for any cosmetic or structural damage to your harp or its component parts as a result of your own attempts to adjust or repair it. If your harp is covered under a manufacturer's warranty, it is possible that any work done to it by someone not authorized or certified by the harp maker may void the warranty. Check the language of the warranty contract or contact your harp maker.

That said, there is no cause for panic. Harp regulation focuses primarily on the mechanical parts of the instrument - the levers, strings, bridge pins, and tuning pins - and most of the time these parts can be replaced even if they are damaged beyond repair. There is a chance that a wrong move with a tool such as a screwdriver will result in a scratch, dent, or other cosmetic damage to your instrument. This kind of damage can be repaired by a finish touch-up expert if needed.

It is also important that the harp be in good structural condition prior to making any adjustments. If your harp has any cracks or separations that could compromise its integrity, attempts to regulate it may be unsuccessful and may worsen the problem. Consult a professional before following other instructions in this book. Even if the harp appears to be in good condition, it would be wise to have it inspected before attempting to regulate it, especially if it is more than ten years old and has not been serviced in five years or more.

Definitions: Sharp, Flat, and Natural

Discussing levers and how they affect a harp's tuning can quickly become confusing because the words flat, natural, and sharp are used in a couple of different ways. First, there is the pitch of a string as tuned. For instance, a G string on the harp can be tuned to G♭, G♮, or G♯, depending on the key and the needs of the piece being played. These are often referred to as note spellings. Second, there is the distinction between notes produced by a string with the lever engaged or disengaged. Levers are often called "sharping" levers, since their function is to raise a string's pitch one half-step higher (i.e., sharper).

It is important to remember that when a lever is engaged, the string can be said to be "sharped," but the resulting pitch may not be a "♯". If the open string is tuned to A♭, for instance, the sharped pitch will be A♮. If the open string is tuned to A♮, then the sharped pitch will be A♯.

In order to speak more generically about the sharping action of a lever without regard to the spelling of the particular notes involved, I will refer to the pitch of a string with the lever disengaged as the "open" string or pitch, and with the lever engaged as the "sharped" string or pitch.

If you are new to music, and all this talk of flats and sharps is giving you a headache, see Appendix A for a crash course in musical notation before reading further.

Chapter Two

Knowing Your Harp

Parts of the Lever Harp

While regulation is primarily concerned with strings and levers, unwanted noises can originate from elsewhere on the instrument, so it is best that we establish a common vocabulary of the various parts referred to on a harp. Figure 2-1 shows a typical lever harp.

The strings are anchored inside the body and pass through holes in the soundboard. They are wound around tuning pins in the neck. The neck also holds the bridge pins and levers.

Playing one or more strings causes them to vibrate, which in turn causes vibrations in the soundboard. The body is a hollow chamber which amplifies the vibrations from the soundboard. The forepillar connects the neck to the body, and provides structural support against the tension of the strings. The forepillar is also frequently referred to as the column, especially in pedal harps or in lever harps that more closely resemble pedal harps, such as the Lyon & Healy Prelude or Salvi Ana.

Figure 2-2 shows a close-up of a lever harp neck. Each string is wound around a tuning pin. A bridge pin defines the speaking length of the string, the portion that vibrates and produces sound. The remainder of the string, the part between the bridge pin and tuning pin, is referred to as the non-speaking length. While it does vibrate when played, the sound is so high-pitched and quiet that it is not audible to the player or the audience.

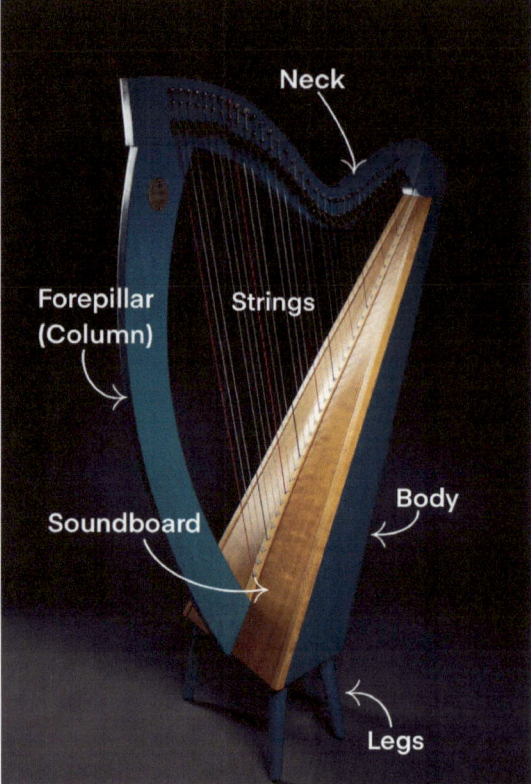

Figure 2-1. A typical lever harp with major structural parts labeled

On the harp shown here, each string has a corresponding lever. Not all lever harps have a full set of levers. Some will be partially levered, saving some expense while still allowing the harp to be played in several common keys.

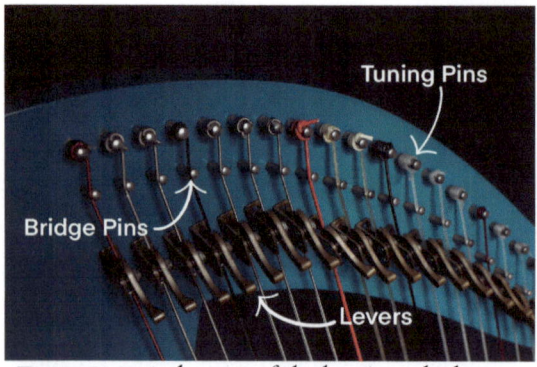

Figure 2-2. A close up of the harp's neck showing tuning pins, bridge pins, and levers

In addition to the harp pictured in Figures 2-1 and 2-2, I used a two string demonstration "harp" to make some of the close up photos possible. It has worked well, as it is difficult to get a close view of an individual lever on a fully levered harp. I must confess that since it is only a wooden board with strings, it doesn't have much of a sound! (See Figure 2-3).

Regulation Theory

The main goal of a regulation is to position the lever so that when it is engaged it raises the pitch of the corresponding string by exactly one half-step. So how is this accomplished? Let's look at the factors that govern lever position.

When we engage a lever, we change the string's pitch by changing its speaking length. An engaged lever makes the string shorter, thus raising the pitch. In order to raise the pitch by the correct amount, the lever must be in the correct location relative to the string's length (Figure 2-4).

Figure 2-3. A two string "harp" used for some of the photographs in this book.

In some levers, including the Loveland, there are other factors which also affect intonation, including the string's distance from the neck. We will discuss these in detail, but for now, just consider the change in speaking length.

When a harp is made, the harp maker locates holes for the levers that will place them in the correct positions. Once the levers are installed on the harp, the levers are adjusted to fine-tune the relationship between the natural and sharp speaking lengths. Over time, with slight changes to the harp's shape as we discussed earlier, the levers need to be adjusted periodically to compensate. All levers have a vertical slot for the screw that fastens them to the neck. The slot allows the lever to be moved up and down as needed (Figure 2-5).

Firgure 2-4. The lever on the left is disengaged. The one on the right is engaged, shortening the string's speaking length.

A given string's intonation is checked by carefully tuning the string with the lever disengaged, then engaging the lever and checking the string's tuning. If the sharped pitch is sharper or flatter than a perfect half-step, the speaking length of the sharped pitch needs to be adjusted to correct this, as we'll go over in detail in Chapter 7.

Lever Harp Tunings

Lever harps can be tuned to a variety of different scales depending on the owner's preference or recommendation of a teacher. Common keys for lever harp tuning are C major, Eb major, F major, and Bb major. The simplest scale, of course, is C major. Since it has no sharps and flats, it is the easiest to read on the tuner, and the easiest to think about conceptually. It is often recommended for beginning harpists for this reason. Since there are no flats in C major, however, engaging the levers to change keys can only result in keys that involve sharps in their key signatures, such as G, D, A, and E, among others.

Slot

Figure 2-5. A slot for the mounting screw allows the lever to be adjusted vertically to optimize intonation.

In order to play a key that includes flats, some of the strings need to be tuned flat. For example, you cannot reach the key of F major if your harp is tuned to C major, because there is no way to lower the the B string to play a Bb. If you tune to the key of Eb major, you can easily reach F major by engaging the Eb and Ab levers. Additionally, from Eb, you are still able to play in the keys of G, D, E, and A major. So, while Bb major and F major are also used regularly, due to its versatility, Eb major is the most common tuning for lever harps. Figures 2-6-2-8 show some of the most common keys.

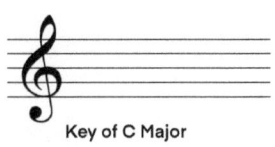

Key of C Major

Figure 2-6. The key of C Major

As a harpist, you are probably well aware of what key your harp is tuned to. If you are regulating a harp that is not your own, the first thing you should do is determine what key it is tuned to. You can ask the owner or simply play the strings and determine the tonic note of the scale. One of the first steps in the regulation process we will discuss later is to check that the tuning pins are tight. Doing this can put them out of tune, so it is important to establish the harp's key before doing any work.

If you are new to the harp, all this talk of flats may cause you confusion when you try to tune, because you won't see any flat notes listed on your electronic tuner. Tuners generally list only natural and sharp notes. To tune a flat note, you will have to read it on the tuner as its enharmonic equivalent. For instance, to tune a string to B♭, tune it to read A♯. If the term "enharmonic equivalent" is new to you, or if you need a refresher, turn to Appendix A for an explanation.

Key of F Major

Figure 2-7. The key of F Major

A harp that is regulated in one key should sound good if tuned to another. While the change in tension on certain strings caused by tuning to a different key technically alters a string's intonation, my experience in practice is that this alteration is not noticeable to most people. Nevertheless, it is a good practice to regulate a harp in whichever tuning is most preferred by the player.

Key of E Flat Major

Figure 2-8. The key of E flat Major

Chapter Three

The Loveland Lever

There are a number of different sharping levers available in the United States and around the world. This book deals exclusively with regulating the Loveland lever. Made by the Loveland Harp Company, they are a popular choice among American harp makers. If you aren't certain what type of levers your harp has, several popular levers are pictured in Figure 3-1. You can also check with the harp maker.

Figure 3-1. From left to right: A Lyon & Healy Performance Lever, and Salvi Lever, and a Loveland Lever

Parts of the Loveland Lever

The Loveland lever, when engaged, changes the speaking length of a string by pinching it between two points: a fret, which is fixed to the lever, and a cam, which can be pivoted up or down to engage or disengage the lever.

Figure 3-2 shows a photo of a typical Loveland lever with its major parts labeled.

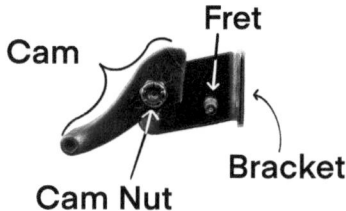

Figure 3-2

The bracket, made of brass, connects with a screw to the harp's neck, securing the lever to the harp. The cam, mounted on a threaded rod, and secured by a nut, can pivot up or down to engage or disengage the string. When raised, the cam pushes the string against the fret, shortening the string's speaking length and thus making it sharper. Some Loveland levers, used on the harp's highest strings, do not have frets, and rely on pressure from the cam alone to change the string's length (figure 3-3). We will look at this in more detail later on.

Each cam has a groove at the point where it pushes the string. Proper lever function depends on that groove matching the string's diameter as closely as possible. Figure 3-4 shows two cams with two different groove sizes.

If the groove is larger than the string's diameter, the string can move within the groove, which often translates to a muddy or buzzy sound. If the groove is too small for the string, the cam can be difficult to engage. Each cam has a small number on its side, which corresponds to the size of this groove. The larger the number, the wider the groove.

The grooves are numbered between #00 and #14. Figure 3-5a shows a #7 cam. The numbers are quite small and difficult to see. Figure 3-5b shows a magnified view of the number stamp. As can be seen in the photo, the numbers are not always stamped right side up.

There are three different bracket sizes on Loveland levers, each of which accommodates a range of cams. Cams designed to fit a given bracket share common dimensions (other than groove size), so there are large, medium, and small cams corresponding to the large, medium, and small brackets (Figure 3-6).

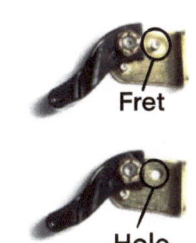

Figure 3-3. The top lever has a fret. The bottom does not. Note the hole in the bracket where the fret was not installed.

Figure 3-4. Two cams viewed from above. Note the larger groove in the tip of the cam at right.

Note that in the different bracket and cam sizes, the position of the fret on the bracket varies, as does the distance between the end of the cam and the fret. The large lever has more space in order to allow for the greater vibrating footprint of a longer, lower string. The small lever needs less space to fit a much smaller string, and the distance it displaces the string when engaged is decreased for better intonation.

Figure 3-5a. A large lever with a #7 cam. The number is visible to the left of the nut.

There are a few other differences found in Loveland levers which are stylistic and do not affect function. As the photos below show, cams are available in black and bronze colors, and the choice of color is up to the harp maker (Figure 3-7). Cams are also available in shorter and longer styles (Figure 3-8). Finally, the cams themselves have been redesigned over time, resulting in differences in feel and look (Figure 3-9). The old and new cams are interchangeable, so if an old one needs to be replaced, a new one will work just fine.

Figure 3-5b. Close up of the number 7 stamped on the cam

Each bracket is fastened to the harp by means of a screw. While a variety of different screws could conceivably be used, the industry standards are hex head screws of various types. Instead of the more common Phillips or slot head, the hex screw's head has a hexagonal shape that accepts an Allen wrench or ball driver (more on these in the next section). The length of the screw used varies by harp maker preference. One half, five eighths, and three-quarter inch screws are all used. There are also two different thread specifications used by different makers, and we'll explore this issue in more detail later as well. Each screw assembly also includes a brass washer, as shown in Figure 3-10.

*Figure 3-6. Top to bottom: large,
medium, and small brackets*

*Figure 3-7. Cams are available in
gold and black.*

Figure 3-8. Top to bottom: a short cam and a long cam

Figure 3-9. The new cam design. Compare these to the older cams in Figure 3-7.

The Bridge Pin

The type of bridge pin used on a harp with Loveland levers also plays a role in the regulation process. The bridge pin is installed in a hole that is deeper than its length, so that it can be driven in deeper over time. The depth of the pin affects the degree to which the lever deflects the string when engaged. As we'll see, this affects the intonation of the engaged string.

Traditionally, bridge pins were "press fit" into their holes. This simply means the hole is tight enough to hold the pin in position, but if sufficient force is applied, it can be pushed in deeper (or pulled out) as needed, to accommodate changes in the harp over time. Many harps are still made this way. More recently, Dusty Strings Harp & Hammered Dulcimer Makers developed a threaded bridge pin meant for use with Loveland levers. It has a hex-shaped head that can be adjusted by means of a wrench. This allows for more accurate adjustment of pin depth. Figure 3-11 shows several different types of bridge pin.

Figure 3-11. Various bridge pins. The first four are press fit. The fifth is threaded.

Chapter Four

Tools Needed

L oveland lever regulation requires a limited number of tools. Some of these will easily be found at any hardware store; others will need to be ordered online. One important tool will need to be made or improvised, as we'll discuss shortly. Since website addresses can change, and companies offering a particular tool now may no longer offer it by the time you read this book, no specific suppliers or URL's will be listed in this book. Searching for the tools by name should enable you to find a list of current sources for them.

You will of course need a tuning key that fits your harp, as well as an electronic tuner.

If you own and play a harp you will already have these on hand, though if you have an inexpensive tuner, you may want to consider an upgrade. The strobe tuners often used by professionals can cost hundreds of dollars and are likely overkill for your needs, but if you have one, by all means use it. There are software versions of these tuners that are available for

Figure 4-1. A tuning key that fits the harp shown in this book.

mobile devices that work quite well and have become the industry standard for professional harpists and technicians alike. They are also incredibly affordable when compared with their hardware counterparts.

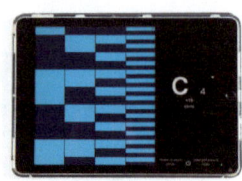

Figure 4-2. Virtual strobe tuning software displayed on a tablet

The tools needed for all Loveland lever setups are a 1/4" wrench (see Figure 4.3) and the appropriate size ball-end screwdriver.

A ball-end driver is hex-shaped, similar to an Allen wrench, but its tip is rounded to facilitate use from odd angles (see Figure 4-4).

Most harps require a 7/64" driver. If your harp was made by Lyon & Healy, however, you will need a 3/32" driver (see Figure 4-5).

You will also need tools to adjust the bridge pins, depending on which type of pin is installed on your harp.

If it is the press fit type, you will need a small hammer and a brass or wooden punch. An eight-ounce ball-peen hammer works great, as does a carpet tack hammer. If all you have is a regular claw hammer, these will work as well, but since you will never use the claw side on a harp, it tends to get in the way.

Figure 4-3. A 1/4" wrench for adjusting cam nuts

For the punch, you will need a piece of wood or metal about one-half inch in diameter and about three inches long. Brass is the best material if you have the tools to cut it to the right size. If not, a very hard wood such as maple should work, though it won't last as long. I do not recommend harder metals, such as steel, which can damage the bridge pins. Figure 4-6 shows the author's ball-peen hammer and brass punch.

Figure 4-4. Ball drivers

Figure 4-5. An Allen wrench (left) has a straight tip while a ball driver (right) has a rounded one.

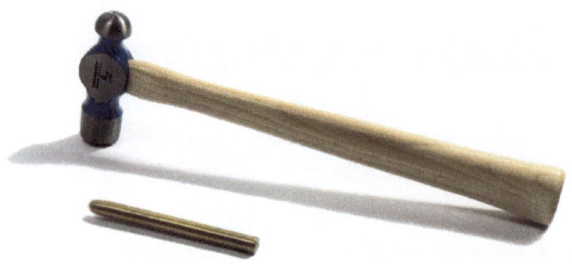

Figure 4-6. An 8 oz. ball peen hammer and a punch made of brass rod

If your harp has the Dusty Strings threaded pins, you will need two nut drivers in sizes 3/16" and 5/32" (Figure 4-7), as well as a special offset wrench that is used only on the top few pins (Figure 4-8). Threaded pins from Robinson's Harp Shop take a 4mm nut driver.

Figure 4-7a. nut drivers used for threaded bridge pins

Figure 4-7b. This angle shows the hexagonal shapes of the nut drivers.

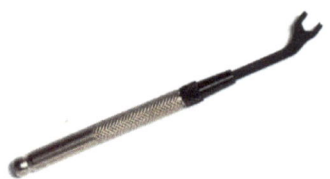

Figure 4-8. An offset wrench used to adjust the top few threaded pins on a Dusty Strings harp

Figure 4-9. A tack puller used to pull out press fit bridge pins when necessary

While most of the time you will be driving bridge pins deeper with the hammer and punch, you will sometimes need to pull one out, especially if you accidentally drive one in too far. For this, a tack lifter comes in handy (see Figure 4-9).

While these normally come with round shafts, yours will need to be flat on its back edge. You can flatten it on a belt sander, with a rotary tool's grinding wheel, or by filing or sanding by hand. Figure 4-10 shows a tack lifter with the back of its shaft ground flat.

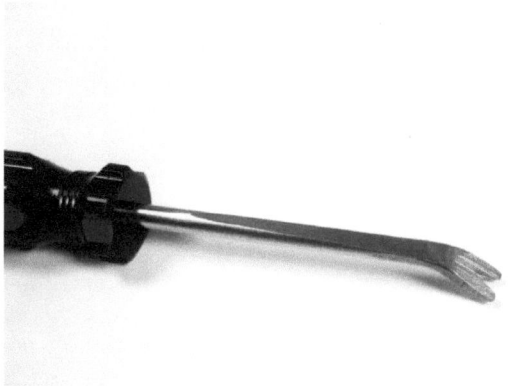

Figure 4-10. Grind the back of the tack puller's shaft
on a belt sander or by hand with a file until it is flat.

In addition to these tools, several others will come in handy. You should have screwdrivers that fit any screw you can find in an accessible location on your harp, especially the feet and legs. Any two parts that are screwed together can become loose and create noise when the harp is played. The specific tools needed will vary by harp. Slot head or Phillips head screws and hex key types (tightened with Allen wrenches) are the most common. If your harp was made outside the US, the correct driver sizes may be metric. It's worth checking with the harp maker for specifications. A small pair of needle-nose pliers, preferably toothless, can also come in handy for aligning parts.

It is advisable to have one or two extra bridge pins in each size and type your harp uses, in case any are damaged during the regulation process.

Chapter Five

Setup

The Importance of String Condition

W hile regulation primarily involves adjusting levers and other small parts, the importance of good strings to the harp's overall sound must not be ignored. Many harpists only replace strings when they break, which can result in a few that stay on the harp far beyond their useful life spans. Over time and with use, strings wear away, becoming thinner in the middle where the harpist plays them. Nylon and gut strings lose their elasticity, giving them a duller, thumpier sound. Dirt and grime build up between the windings of bass strings, which detracts from their tone and sustain. Strings can go "false" when damage or wear throws off their vibration patterns, causing them to sound out of tune no matter how many attempts are made to tune them. Even the best regulation will not fix problems caused by old and worn strings. It is a good idea to replace all of the strings on the harp periodically. How often depends on how much the harp is played, the player's touch, and the materials the strings are made of. If you haven't restrung the harp since you bought it, I would encourage you to try doing so. After the initial annoying period of constant tuning a new set of strings requires, you will no doubt rediscover how wonderful your harp sounded when you first bought it. In general, I recommend a complete restringing every five to eight years, depending on frequency of playing.

The strings also wear away over time at the point where they are engaged by the levers, and this can affect regulation, especially in the harp's top two octaves.

This wear may not be easily seen, so again it is advisable to invest in new strings to get the best regulation possible.

General Maintenance

An important component of any harp regulation should be making sure that screws or joints that hold the instrument and its parts together are tight and that all moving parts are working properly. Lay the harp on a bed or couch so that you can see underneath it. Check any screws you find underneath, including those for legs, leg brackets, or rubber feet. Screws should be tight. If you feel them moving, tighten them, but don't overdo it. Forcing a screw that is already doing its job well can damage it or strip the hole it sits in. If you run across any stripped screws, see Appendix B for repair instructions.

The pillar is likely secured to the body by a screw or bolt. Check that this is tight if you have access to it. There may also be large screws underneath the body, helping to secure the integrity of the base frame.

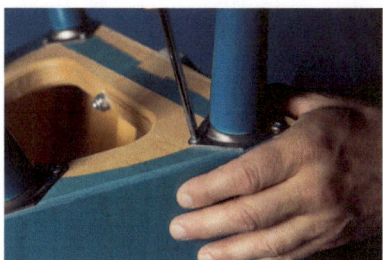

If your harp has a brass plate over the joint between neck and pillar, check the screws there, as well as any nameplates or serial number plates attached to the body. These

Figure 5-1. Tighten screws, including any leg brackets.

connections can all be a source of noise if allowed to become loose.

Tuning Pins

In order to stay in tune, a harp's tuning pins must be secure in their holes. Most lever harps use tapered tuning pins that are smaller in diameter on the string side, and larger on the back end. The holes bored into the neck are tapered to match them. The more tightly the pin is pushed into the hole, the tighter the pin will feel,

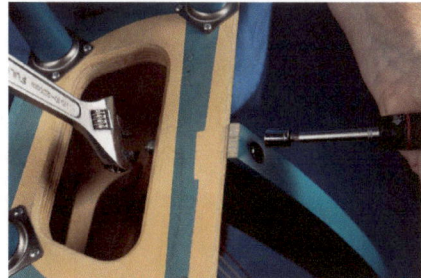

Figure 5-2. Tighten any screws or bolts that fasten the pillar to the body.

and the better it will hold the string's pitch. The pins can work loose in the holes, either because seasonal dryness in the environment shrinks the wood, or because the pins have been turned extensively, such as during restringing. Check all of the pins for tightness. If any feel too loose or are not reliably keeping a string at pitch, tighten them. Brace your left hand against the neck on the string side, and with the tuning key in your right hand, wiggle the pin clockwise and counterclockwise while pushing toward the neck. This will work the pin deeper into the hole and help it hold better.

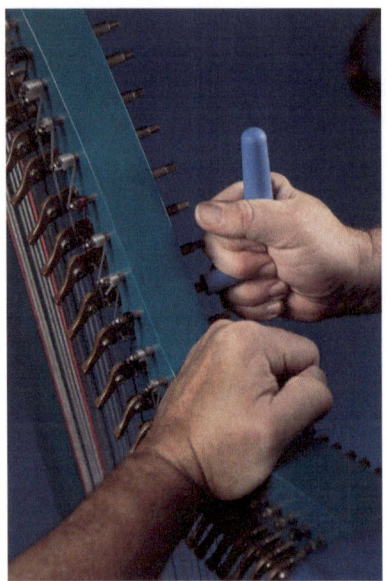

Figure 5-3. Tightening tapered tuning pins

There are a few other tuning pin designs which are handled differently. The tuning pins on Dusty Strings harps made in 1998 and later have fine threading, and are pressed into a straight hole rather than a tapered one. Since the company also makes these available to other makers, you may find them on a different brand of harp as well. They can be distinguished from tapered pins by the shape of the string side, which is slightly smaller in diameter than the shaft that runs through the neck (Figure 5-4). These pins generally stay tight without maintenance, but if you do discover a loose one, it is best to contact a technician rather than repair it yourself.

Figure 5-4. A tapered tuning pin (top) and a Dusty Strings straight tuning pin (bottom)

Zither pins are common on small lap harps. They don't run all the way through the neck, and as a result are tuned from the same side the strings are on. These pins are screwed into the neck. A slightly loose zither pin can sometimes be made firmer by screwing it a turn or two deeper into the neck. If that fails, the hole is likely stripped. See Appendix B for more information on dealing with stripped holes.

Finally, Paraguayan-style and other Central and South American harps use geared tuners similar to those used on guitars and other fretted stringed instruments. A thorough discussion of these tuners is outside the scope of this book. If you have this type of tuners and are experiencing problems keeping your harp in tune, a local luthier or guitar technician may be able to help you, as these tuners are similar to those used on guitars.

Figure 5-5. Zither pins are used on some lap harps.

In addition to tuning pin tightness, check for strings that have wound too many times around the pin. Figure 5-6 shows an example.

Pins with too many windings, especially in the range between middle C and the bass wires, can be very hard to turn, and in some cases their square ends can shear off, making tuning impossible. Strings with too many windings are also more prone to breakage. If you encounter this situation, you can unwind the string completely, pull it through the pin hole so that it is taut, then re-tune the string, as shown in Figures 5-7 through 5-9. Begin by loosening the string until there are no coils left on the pin. Then, pull the end of the string through the hole in the pin as shown in Figure 5-8. Don't pull it completely tight. When you tighten the sting back up, you will want to wind up with two or three coils left. I usually pull the string through the hole until it is tight, then let it back down about one half of an inch.

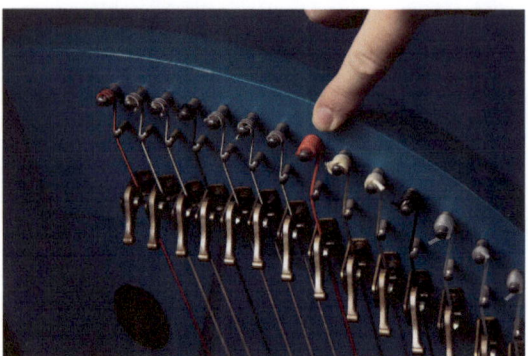

Figure 5-6. A string wound too many times around a tuning pin

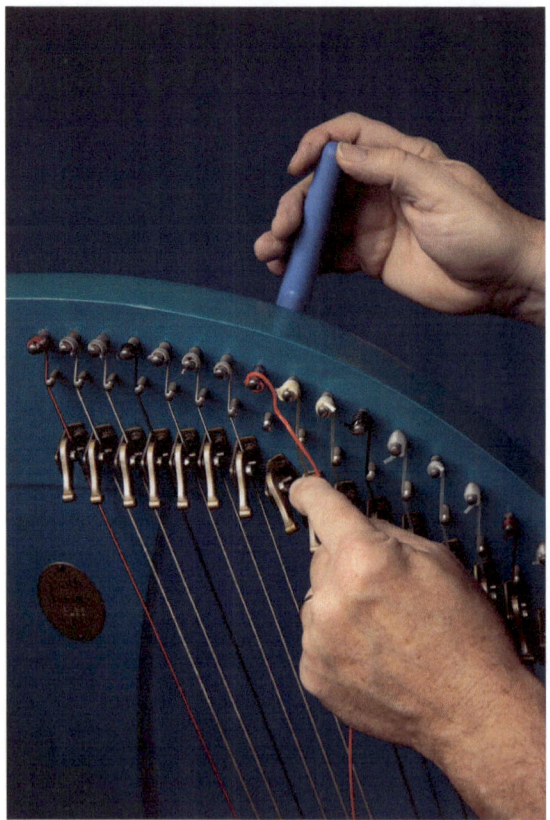

Figure 5-7. Loosen the string until all of the coils have come off the tuning pin.

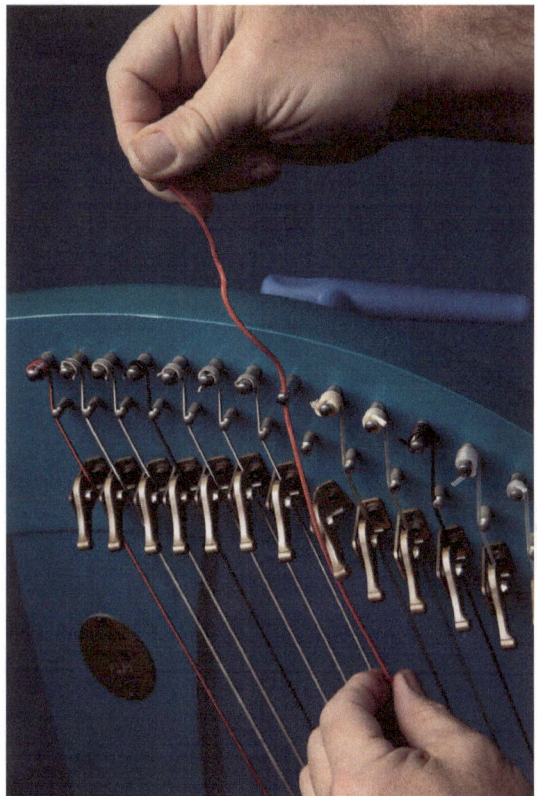

Figure 5-8. Pull the string through the tuning pin to eliminate excess windings.

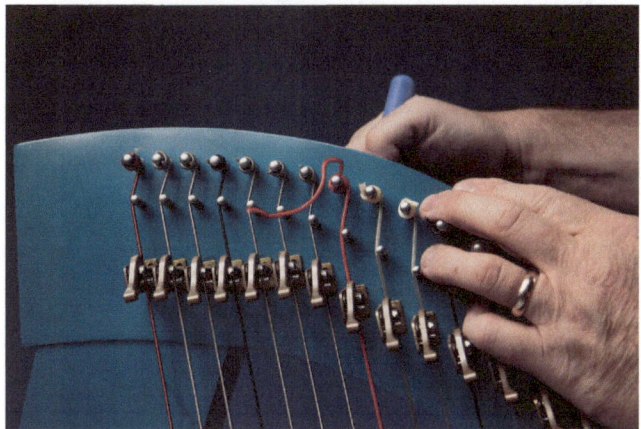

Figure 5-9. Re-tune the string. Since the tension was temporar-ily removed, it will need to be tuned several times before holding pitch well.

Levers

The lever brackets are screwed to the wood by a hex head screw. Each of these should be checked, and tightened if necessary. At the same time, inspect each lever for proper alignment with the string. Ideally, the cam will be parallel to the string, and when the lever is engaged, the lever groove and the string will meet. In practice, this is not always the case. Sometimes a lever needs to be turned at a slight angle relative to the string, in order to ensure that the groove in the cam lines up with the string .

Firgure 5-10. The angles of the levers can be adjusted by loosening the screw holding them to the neck, rotating them, then tightening the screw. Loose cams can be tightened by tightening the nut on the right side of the cam with a 1/4" wrench.

Occasionally you may run into a lever that cannot be lined up satisfactorily with the string. The alignment will be so poor that the string makes a loud "ping" when the lever is engaged, or the lever won't engage it at all. Check to see if the cause is any bent or damaged parts, and replace them yourself or contact a professional. If the parts are not damaged, it is possible that the hole for the lever screw was not properly located when the lever was installed, and the hole should be relocated. That repair is beyond the scope of this book, and I would recommend enlisting professional assistance.

The cams are secured to the brackets by a nut on the right side of the cam. Over time, these nuts can work loose. To check the tightness of each cam, use the quarter-inch wrench and turn it clockwise. It should be tight enough so that it can't fall down inadvertently or rattle sympathetically, but not so tight that it is hard for the player to move up and down. It is also good if all of the cams have a consistent feel. If you over-tighten a cam, you can easily turn it back in the other direction.

When all of these preliminary steps are performed--pins and brackets are tight, structural connections are firm, and lever cams are properly adjusted--you are ready to begin the regulation.

Chapter Six

Noise Control

If you've gone through all of the general maintenance and setup procedures described earlier, you may already have rid your harp of a number of annoying buzzes and rattles, and likely stopped some others that would have developed in the future. Some of the loudest unwanted noises are caused by loose screws in legs and feet or loose levers. Nevertheless, as part of a good regulation you will want to play each string on the harp, with the levers both engaged and disengaged, and check for and eliminate (or at least subdue) any further unwanted sounds.

I tend to categorize noises in two broad groups: attack noises and sympathetic noises. Attack noises are directly related to the string being played or its connected hardware (lever, bridge pin, etc.). Generally speaking, this type of noise will make the note you are playing sound bad. It might lack sustain or sound muddy. It might start off okay but then make a loud rattle. The second type, the sympathetic noise, is a buzz somewhere else in the harp, other than the string being played. As you play the harp, the vibration of the strings causes the soundboard, and to some extent the whole instrument, to vibrate. If anything on the harp is loose that should be tight, its vibration may cause unwanted noise. Sympathetic noises sound different from attack noises in that the string being played may sound normal, but there is a second sound that is not. Sympathetic noises often start a moment or two after the string is played. As you check for and work on fixing noises, know that it is sometimes hard to tell whether a noise is attack-related or sympathetic. It is not required that you know which is which right off the bat. Learning to hear the difference is merely a tool that can help you identify and fix a problem more efficiently.

When regulating a harp, I play each string several times fairly loudly. If there is a noise problem, it is mostly likely to be heard during a forte or fortissimo passage. Don't overplay, however, or you will tend to hear problems that would never occur during normal music-making. Play through each string on the harp, first with the levers disengaged, then again with all of the levers engaged. When I run across a noise that needs attention, I stop and troubleshoot it, fixing it before moving on to the rest of the strings. It would be equally valid to make a note of the issue, play through the rest of the strings, then come back and fix any problems later.

Figure 6-1. A threaded bridge pin. Note hexagonal shape

If you detect an unwanted noise, the next step is to isolate it. This can be more difficult than you might expect. Since a harp is built to amplify and transmit sound, unwanted noises can "travel" around the instrument. A high-pitched sympathetic vibration coming from inside the body, for instance, can sound like it is coming from somewhere on the neck. To isolate a noise, your ears and hands need to work together. Moving your ear around to different parts of the harp to listen for where the noise is louder can give a clue to its origin. With your hands, you can stop certain parts from vibrating to hear if the noise stops, which can also help you locate the source. We will go over specifics shortly. Just keep in mind the general need to locate and isolate any noise you are trying to deal with.

Attack Buzzes, Lever Disengaged

Figure 6-2. A press fit bridge pin is round in shape.

If a string buzzes with the lever disengaged, the most common issue is that the string is hitting some part of the lever. The string passes between the lever's cam and its fret. If it is too close to either one, it may bump into it when played, causing an unpleasant sound. This problem is most common on the lowest strings, where the amount of space is small compared to the long string's fairly large arc of vibration. For the lowest ten strings or so, the string should be equidistant between the cam and the fret, giving it the maximum possible amount of space to vibrate. As a harp ages, slight warpage of the pillar and neck may skew the string more toward the cam, and the bridge pin will need to be driven or screwed in slightly. It is unlikely to find a low string that is too close to the fret unless it was adjusted incorrectly.

You will occasionally run into a press fit pin that is loose in its hole, and the string tension pushes it too far in. Correcting this problem is beyond the scope of this book.

As you move up through the strings, you should see each one set up closer and closer to the fret. As we'll see in the section on intonation, we generally want each string to be set up as close to the fret as possible without buzzing. As the length and diameter of the strings decrease, they can be set closer and closer to the fret without the risk

Figure 6-3. Adjusting a threaded bridge pin with a nut driver

of buzzing, until on the high strings they can look like they are practically touching it.

To change the string's distance from the fret, use the tools appropriate to the type of bridge pin you have. For the threaded type, adjust it with the nut driver.

Turn it only slightly before checking the string for noise again. It is easy to go too far.

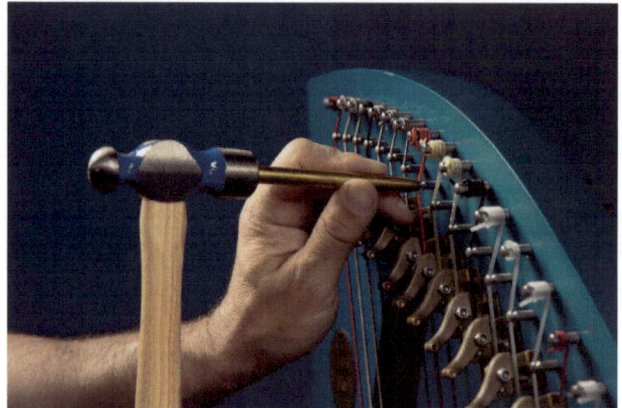

Figure 6-4. Adjusting a press fit bridge pin with a hammer and punch

If your harp has press fit bridge pins, you drive them deeper by placing the brass punch against them, then tapping the punch with your hammer, as shown in Figure 6-4. Do not use the hammer directly on the pin, because the pins are so close together that it will be impossible to hit only one, and you risk hitting other parts and damaging them.

Be very conservative when driving a bridge pin deeper. It is harder to get them back out if you go too far, so tap lightly, then check, then tap again if necessary. You will develop a feel for how much force is needed to move the pins on your harp.

Figure 6-5. The bridge pin for this G string has been driven to far in. The string may hit the fret when played.

If a pin is too close to a fret (or if you accidentally set it too close), as shown in Figure 6-5, you'll need to pull it out with your tack puller. The procedure for this is to brace the V-shaped notch in the pin's string groove. Set the shaft against the head of a nearby tuning pin as a fulcrum.

This is why I mentioned the shaft must be flattened in the section on tools. If it is round, it will not sit steadily on the tuning pin. Place your tuning key on the other side of the same pin as shown in Figure 6-6. You are using the tuning pin as a fulcrum, and the tack puller as a lever. Gently pry the bridge pin out. As you pry you will be pressing the tuning pin toward the neck, and it will work loose if you don't apply pressure in the opposite direction with your right hand.

Pulling a press fit pin out as described here is not easy. It takes some hand and arm strength to properly brace the tools. Even if done correctly, it can damage the string groove of the pin. You will want to avoid driving pins in too far. If you get stuck pulling one out, you will quickly develop a distaste for doing so, and learn to drive them in conservatively!

If you damage the pin's groove, there's a good chance of a sharp edge that will cause string breakage. It is best to replace the pin with a new one if this happens.

You may also run across a pin that needs to be driven deeper, but refuses to budge. It is most likely in this case that the pin is "bottomed out", meaning it has hit the bottom of the hole and can't go any deeper. The only options here are to make the hole deeper or the pin shorter. The hole must be the correct diameter or the pin will be too loose, so here, too, I advise that you get a professional involved.

Figure 6-6. Pulling out a press fit bridge pin with a tack puller. A nearby tuning pin is used as a fulcrum. Be sure to brace that pin with your other hand and a tuning key.

Attack Buzzes, Lever Engaged

If the buzz occurs with the lever engaged, a quick way to determine if the lever itself is involved is to play the string with one hand while bracing the thumb or finger of your other hand on the lever. If the noise changes or disappears, the lever or cam may be loose. Double check the screws securing the bracket to the harp and the nut that tensions the cam. If neither of these are loose, check the tip of the cam for breakage. Pieces can break off, usually in older levers, causing the lever to lose its hold on the string (Figure 6-7). This is most common on higher strings. If there is damage to the cam it will need to be replaced. See Appendix C for instructions on cam replacement.

Figure 6-7. A cam with a corner chipped off can cause a buzz or twangy sound.

If none of these fixes works, there is a chance the groove in the cam is too large. As we discussed earlier, the small number stamped on each cam refers to the diameter of the cam's string groove. The smaller the number, the smaller the groove. Replacing a cam with the next number size down can eliminate a buzz when all else fails. I have run into a number of cases where the original lever placed on a harp seems to have too large a cam groove and needs to be downsized. I assume that the string did not buzz when the harp was first sold, but perhaps the original cam had little margin for error, and some wear and tear enlarged it just a little. It is also possible that the string is not exactly the same as the string used on the harp when it was first made, and doesn't work well with the lever cam's groove. In either case, replacing the cam with one the next size down usually takes care of it.

Downsizing the cam groove can make the lever feel tighter when engaging and disengaging. In my opinion, this is a good trade-off for eliminating the buzz.

Sympathetic buzzes

If none of the ideas above fixes the problem, you may have a sympathetic buzz. It is important to note whether the buzz occurs with the lever engaged or disengaged, not because the lever is necessarily involved but because the sympathetic vibration generally happens at a particular pitch or small range of pitches. If you have a buzz on your middle C♯, for instance, something on the harp is vibrating audibly at that exact pitch. The trick is locating that "something." The general procedure for tracking down a sympathetic buzz is playing the problem note repeatedly while damping various parts of the instrument with your other hand. If placing your hand somewhere stops the buzz, you've narrowed down its location. Enlisting a helper can also be useful. One person can play the string while the other searches for the source of the noise.

Here are some common buzz causes.

Another string/lever. Playing one string on the harp results in the sympathetic vibration of many strings. The most prominent ones will be related to your problem string by octaves (assuming their lever positions are all the same as the one you're playing, and the harp is in tune). If you hear a buzz on a string with the lever engaged but can't isolate the sound to that lever, it is possible the lever an octave or two below is buzzing, for instance. As you play the string, damp sections of levers with your other hand to see if the noise goes away. If it does, damp individual levers in that range to isolate the one causing the issue. Tighten or replace as necessary (see Appendix C).

String ends. This is one of the most common sources of sympathetic vibrations. If the tails of the string knots underneath the soundboard are too long, two might be close enough to touch, and will make a noise when playing makes them vibrate. String knots should be clipped as short as possible to avoid this. Even if they are short, though, sometimes a tail can vibrate against an anchor, or the knot itself may be loose enough to buzz. Play the string and put one hand inside the body at the same time, damping groups of strings to try and localize the source. Often, it is not the string you are playing. If you locate a buzz here, cut any long ends. If they are already short, sometimes a buzz will go away with a simple firm push on the knot. You can twist the knot a little to add tension, but no more than a quarter turn to avoid damaging the string. If these approaches fail, the best option is to replace the string that is causing an issue.

Legs and feet. If you haven't done the general maintenance and setup described earlier, a loose part of the harp's leg system could be involved. Check and tighten as necessary.

Accessories. If anything is attached to your harp, such as a holder for a tuning key, a transducer wire, output jack, or decoration, it can buzz. Pickup wires need to be secure and not loose inside the harp's body. They are a common buzzing issue, especially in the lower range.

Foreign objects. I have removed some interesting objects from harps. Small toys, loose change, and writing utensils seem to be the most common. Side note: clipping a mechanical pencil somewhere inside the harp is not a very clever place to keep it!

Room buzzes. The source of the noise may not be your harp at all, but something vibrating nearby. You might swear that the noise is louder with your ear against the harp, but nothing you do affects it. Look around you. What objects might move or rattle? Some of the most common ones I run into are light fixtures and fixture covers. Practice rooms at schools and colleges are notorious for these. Metal window blinds can be loud. Loose heating duct grates, glass curio shelves, harp benches, music stands, the list is long. If you hear the buzz even when you stand as far back as possible while still playing the string, or if a helper plays it while you check the room, then you are likely dealing with a room buzz. Don't overlook the trash can. I can't count the number of times kicking the contents of a metal waste basket miraculously fixed a buzzing harp! A great way to rule out buzzing in a room is to take the harp to another room as far away as possible and check for the buzz. If it is gone, it is coming from the room you started in.

Loose structural parts. If you can stop a buzz by pressing on a particular spot on the harp itself, some part of its structure that should be glued or screwed together may be loose. If you can't locate a screw to tighten, a loose brace or joint might need to be reglued. Contact a professional unless you have a lot of woodworking knowledge.

I couldn't possibly cover every source of noise, but most harp buzzes will be in the list above. If not, the act of looking for these noises may help you stumble onto the real cause. Be patient, tracking down noises can be tedious. But there's nothing like finally figuring out what is happening and eliminating an obnoxious buzz.

Chapter Seven

Intonation

O nce attention has been given to a harp's overall maintenance, and unwanted noises have been eliminated, the final step in the regulation process is to check the intonation. While this word can have a variety of meanings in the contexts of different musical instruments, for harps it refers to whether each lever, when engaged, raises its string's pitch by exactly one half step.

With Loveland levers, two factors influence intonation: the lever's vertical position relative to the string and the distance the lever pushes the string in order to press it against the fret. The vertical position determines the amount the string's speaking length changes, and the distance the lever pushes the string adds additional tension which can influence the sharped string's pitch. In the coming section, I will refer to this as "the degree of deflection", or simply "the deflection". You will sometimes hear it referred to as "grip". This is a term borrowed from pedal harp regulation to describe the same effect of the harp's moving parts exerting tension on the strings. While the term makes perfect sense if you regulate all sorts of different harps, in the context of Loveland levers it doesn't make intuitive sense, so I will avoid it here.

For each levered string on the harp, you can check the intonation by tuning the string to pitch to an electronic tuner with the lever disengaged, then engaging the lever and playing the string again. If the lever is perfectly regulated, the tuner will show the sharped pitch to be in tune as well. If it is a little too high or low, it can be adjusted using the procedures outlined below.

I just used the word "perfectly" in the preceding paragraph. In music, as in many other aspects of life, perfection is a lofty but often unattainable goal. As we regulate in the real world, we will strive for perfection while understanding that the best we can get is a sharped pitch that is as in tune as possible. Most well-made harps can be regulated well enough that they will sound good to most people. Sometimes a harp can be modified to account for a problem with its design, or a lever that was inexpertly installed can be relocated, but once again, those kinds of improvements are beyond the scope of this book. If you'd like to read a discussion of why perfect intonation is an unrealistic expectation in harps, you'll find it in Appendix D.

To briefly review some terms, the words "sharp" and "flat" can be part of note names (as in C♯), but they can also be used to describe the intonation in the harp (as in "the C♯ is a little *too* sharp"). To avoid using these two meanings in the same sentence, I will describe the intonation as "too high", "too low", or "in tune". So instead of "The C♯ is too flat", we'll say "the C♯ is too low". They both mean the same thing, but the latter should be clearer here. It's also correct to say a string is "in regulation" (meaning the sharped pitch is in tune), or "out of regulation" (meaning it is not).

The process of checking intonation involves tuning each string very precisely. You can save time by getting all the strings in good tune to begin with, so I always start this process by tuning the whole harp.

When setting out to check each string and lever, which string on the harp should you start with? While beginning on either the highest or lowest note might seem logical, in practice, neither choice is good. The lowest strings are hard to tune even with high quality electronic tuners. The tuners have trouble reading low notes, and their lights or indicators often jump around. Beginning your regulation while dealing with this challenge gets you started on the wrong foot. For reasons I'll discuss shortly, regulating the lowest notes is often a waste of time.

Starting on the highest note and working down means starting with the trickiest, most temperamental strings first. The shorter a string is, the more even the slightest adjustment will change it, so this section of the harp involves some of the most tedious and slow work in the whole procedure. Sure, you could take an "eat the frog" approach and tackle the toughest part first, looking forward to an easier finish, and there is no reason you can't do it this way if it makes more sense to you. Personally, I find it more efficient to start on an easier section and build momentum to carry me into the more challenging areas. Starting in the middle of the harp, such as at middle C, and working your way down, then returning to middle C and working your way up means you will start where the tuner reads reliably and the adjustments are fairly straightforward. I find myself getting into a rhythm by working quickly through an easier section, and this rhythm helps keep me from bogging down when the going gets harder.

I mentioned above that on the shorter strings, even the most minute adjustment can make a big difference. On the longer strings, the opposite is true. On a bass string, moving a lever as far up or down as it will go, or making the maximum possible alteration in deflection will have little or no effect on the sharped pitch's intonation. While I would encourage you to check the regulation on the lowest octave and a half or so of your own harp, I believe you will find, as I have, that there is little you can do to adjust regulation. Fortunately, unless something went very wrong when the levers were first installed, this area of any harp tends to stay in regulation without any help from a regulator.

For this reason, my standard procedure is to start regulating on the F string below middle C, the 4th octave F. If I am unfamiliar with the model of harp, I will work my way down from there, but I usually find either that the intonation is good, or that there is nothing moving a lever or adjusting a bridge pin will do to make a significant difference. Once I've reached this decision, I return to the 4th octave F and work my way upward.

As you check each string and lever, when you come across one that is not in tune, you will need to adjust the lever up or down, and/or adjust the height of the bridge pin. Focusing on the lever for now, it can be moved by loosening the bracket screw, moving the lever, then tightening the screw (Figure 7-1).

Figure 7–1. Raise a lever to lower the sharped pitch.
Lower a lever to raise the sharped pitch.

If the sharped pitch is too high, moving the lever up will make it lower. This happens because the speaking length of the sharped pitch becomes a little longer, lowering its pitch. Conversely, If the sharped pitch is too low, moving the lever down will raise it. Generally, the shorter the string, the more of a difference each lever move will make in the intonation. As you work on higher and higher strings, try to reduce the amount you move each lever before checking the intonation again.

Deflection, again, refers to the distance the lever cam pushes the string before it stops at the fret. The more deflection, the higher the sharped pitch will be, as deflection adds tension to the string. Driving or screwing the bridge pin deeper into the neck lowers the sharped pitch. Pulling or unscrewing it raises the pitch. Figure 7-2 illustrates this. The difference is slight, but the string on the left is being deflected more than the one on the right, and as a result will be slightly sharper.

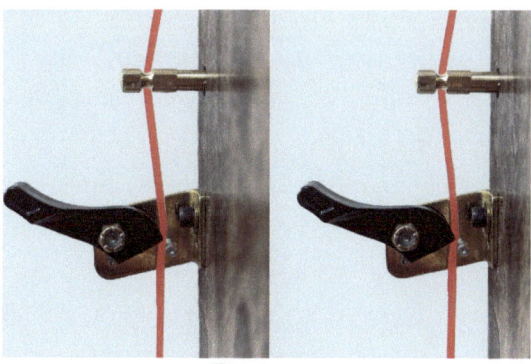

Figure 7-2.

Since two factors control intonation on each string, which one should you focus on first? It depends. Observe the current positions of the lever and bridge pin. Is there room to move the lever in the direction it needs to go? Can the height of the bridge pin be changed without causing the string to be too close to hitting either the fret or the cam? Often, you will find that you have only one option. The lever may be as high as it will go, but the bridge pin can be moved, or the opposite may be true. In those cases, the decision is simple.

If you can go either way, the question is, how much of a change do you need to make? Moving the lever tends to cause a more drastic change; adjusting the bridge pin makes a more subtle difference. If the interval just needs a tweak, a fine adjustment to the bridge pin is in order. If it is significantly off, moving the lever first should get it into the ballpark, where it can be fine-tuned by adjusting the bridge pin.

Always use caution when driving a press fit bridge pin deeper, to avoid driving it too deep, which can cause the string to hit the fret when played. While the pin can be pulled out, that is more difficult and time-consuming than driving it in, and the process can result in damage to the pin. For this reason, lowering a high sharped pitch by pulling out a press fit bridge pin is always a last resort. When in doubt whether to adjust the lever or pin, it's safer to try the lever first.

To adjust a threaded bridge pin, place the correct size of nut driver over the nut's head and turn clockwise to move the string toward the fret, or counterclockwise to move it toward the cam. Refer back to Figures 4-7 and 4-8 in Chapter 4 for photos of these tools. For a press fit bridge pin, you move it toward the fret by placing your brass punch on its head and tapping the punch with your hammer, as shown earlier in Figure 6-3.

As I mentioned earlier, the top four to six levers often do not have a fret. (See Figure 3-3 for a photo of levers with and without frets) The strings here are short enough that pushing the string all the way to a fret would make it too high. One can still move the levers up or down, but often they will need to be set as high as they can go. The press fit pins can be adjusted in the same way. The amount the cam deflects the string still bears on how high or low the sharped pitch is.

On harps with Dusty Strings threaded pins, the tips on the top few strings are conical, offering no head on which to place the nut driver. This is done to allow the levers room to be set higher than they can be with the standard pins. These are adjusted with an offset wrench, available from Dusty Strings. With this wrench, you can reach behind the string and turn the hex-shaped pin from closer to its base. (See Figure 4-8)

The previous paragraphs outline the general procedure for checking and adjusting intonation. The following tips discuss good habits and techniques to develop, and offer specifics on handling certain situations and areas of the harp.

Keep a hand on the lever. If you are adjusting a lever up or down, hold the lever steady with one hand while loosening the screw with your other hand, in order to control the amount of movement. If you just loosen the screw the lever may fall loose, and you won't know where it was when you started. Trying your best to keep it in place as the screw is loosened helps you control the distance it is moved (see Figure 7-2).

After making any adjustment, check for noise. Sometimes moving a lever can change its alignment, or produce an unwanted noise that wasn't there before.

Play the string repeatedly. As you tune a string, play it more than once. I usually have a slow march tempo in my head as I'm tuning, and play the string on each quarter note. As I tune higher and higher strings, I increase the tempo. This technique helps tune the string accurately by keeping the electronic tuner's attention on the attack of the note you're playing and not any other noise going on in the background. If you just play a string once, the indicator on your tuner might waver quite a bit after the initial attack on the string, making it hard to tell whether it's in tune. On higher strings, there is a decreasing amount of sustain on each attack, so it helps to play more frequently.

Always double-check the open pitch after checking the sharped pitch. If the sharped pitch is in tune, always disengage the lever and check the open pitch to make sure it hasn't wavered and given you a false reading for the sharped pitch. This is especially true on new or fairly new strings (two months old or less). The act of engaging the string with the lever can stretch the string slightly, knocking it out of tune and giving you a misleading reading of the sharped pitch.

Cultivate speed. Once you get an open pitch in tune, the more quickly you can engage the lever and check the sharped pitch, the more accurate your reading will be. This is hard at first, but it is a good goal to increase the accuracy of your regulations. This is not about getting through the job faster or rushing. It's about minimizing the time between tuning the string and judging the intonation of the sharped pitch.

To minimize cosmetic damage, it helps to use both hands when working with your tools: holding the driver or wrench in your dominant hand, use your other hand to guide the tool to its target. I often rest the driver on my thumb near its tip and guide it toward the screw. This helps prevent jabbing the blades of tools somewhere you don't want them.

"Better sharp than out of tune." If you can't get a sharped pitch right where you want it, it is better to err on the side of a slightly wide (too high) interval than a slightly narrow (too low) one. Our ears tend to hear slightly wide intervals as "sweeter" sounding, and slightly narrow ones as dull or less in tune.

Some harp makers who use press fit bridge pins alter them in some way for the highest strings to allow the levers to be raised a little higher. In this register, the levers must be very close to the bridge pins in order to play in tune when sharped. Often you'll see that the bottom half of the tip of each pin has been filed off to allow more room for the lever. These can be adjusted the same way as unaltered pins. On the Dusty Strings threaded pins we just discussed, this is the reason the top few have conical heads. This allows the lever to be raised higher than a standard bridge pin would allow.

Chapter Eight

Conclusion

Having the knowledge and skills to regulate your own lever harp means never having to wait for an out of town technician if you hear that something is not quite right on your instrument. It means you have the tools and knowledge to do minor repairs if the harp gets tipped over just before a gig and you need to straighten out a few levers. It means dealing with small problems before they become big ones, helping you get the most out of your harp year after year.

For all its rewards, harp regulation can be challenging as well as repetitive and tedious. Even an experienced technician may have to adjust an upper register string and pin several times before hitting the right combination. As a novice, you may find yourself re-doing things over and over and feeling that you're only making the problem worse. You'll need to be patient, and be kind to yourself. While the principle of regulation is quite simple, the practice and the manual skills needed can take time to master. After giving this process a try, you may find it's not for you, and there's nothing wrong with that. I'm happy to have your business if you prefer to delegate the job! Even if you ultimately choose not to do this yourself, I'm glad you've stuck with the book this far. Understanding regulation's goals and procedures is valuable for any harp owner.

If you regulate your harp and run into a problem, let me know. I have always made educating and assisting harpists a core function of Moss Harp Service. If you need clarification of an explanation in this text or run into a problem I haven't addressed, contact me through my website at mossharpservice.com.

Chapter Nine

Appendices

Appendix A: Basic Music Information

This appendix provides basic information regarding aspects of music notation and theory that are relevant to tuning and regulating harps. This is by no means a complete or comprehensive introduction to music. If you learned to read music in the past, this appendix should help you brush up on some relevant concepts that will be useful.

If you are new to the harp or to music, or not a musician at all but wish to learn to regulate harps, you will want to supplement this information by taking an online class on reading music, asking your teacher, or searching the internet. Think of this information as an outline to assist you as you gather more information.

The following basics of music notation and theory should not be considered universal. Different cultures throughout history and throughout the world have developed different systems of music. The system described here is of European origin, and is often referred to as "Western" music. It has been adopted quite widely throughout the modern world, but is by no means the only system of theory and notation in use today.

When discussing the basics of music, it is often useful to use the keys of the piano as a visual aide. Most people, musician or not, have seen a piano keyboard, and many of those people have spent at least a little time studying piano, or merely noodling on the keys. For these reasons, I will refer to the piano to some extent here, even though this book is concerned with harp regulation.

Figure A-1 shows a section of a piano keyboard with the white keys labeled with their corresponding letters. Note that the letter C is used twice, both at the beginning and the end. If we were to continue to play the white keys in either direction, all of the letters would be reused. The span of notes between each repeating letter is known as an octave. We refer to these two C notes as being an octave apart. More on octaves shortly. The pattern of keys shown above repeats several times on the

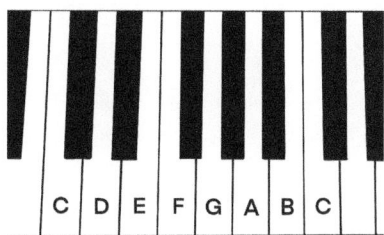

Figure A-1. The white keys of a piano labeled with their note names

piano keyboard, as it is capable of playing several octaves. A pianist learns their way around the keyboard by learning how the arrangement of black and white keys corresponds to different notes.

Figure A-2 shows a section of strings on a harp. Harp strings are color coded to help the harpist navigate the strings. All C strings are colored red and all F strings are colored black or dark blue.

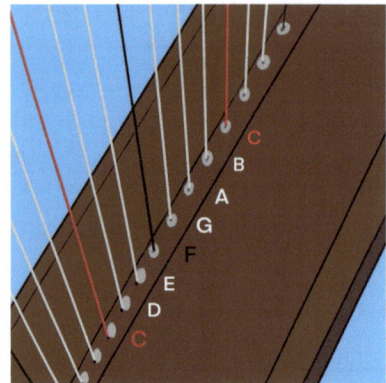

Figure A-2. Harp strings with their note names labeled

Besides having the same name, notes an octave apart have a mathematical relationship. The higher C on the right end of the illustration vibrates at twice the frequency of the one on the left. This relation ship continues up and down the keyboard. Each higher C is twice the frequency of the one before it, and each lower one is half the frequency of the one above it. Because of this relationship, notes an octave part sound very similar in character. If these two C's are played together, it may be hard to tell if one is playing one key or two. Figure A-3 highlights the relationship between notes an octave apart by showing the repeating C's in green. Figure A-4 expands by showing three C's on the keyboard.

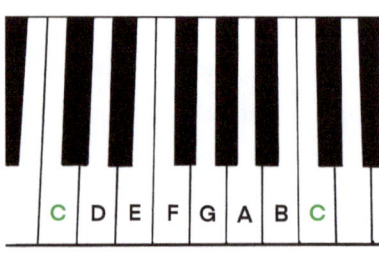

Figure A-3. Two C's one octave apart

Each octave is subdivided into individual notes. While there are seven letters used in musical notation, the octave in Western music is divided into twelve notes, or steps, starting on any given note and ending on the same note an octave above. The notes between a given letter are assigned a sharp or flat symbol that indicates they are one half step higher or lower than the note with the same name. A♯ is one half step higher than A♮, for instance. Letters that are neither sharp nor flat are referred to as natural notes. The "♮" symbol is used to mark a natural pitch, but in many cases you will see a letter name with no symbol, as a note with neither a sharp nor a flat symbol is assumed to be natural.

On the piano keys, the white keys represent all of the natural notes, and the black keys represent the sharps and flats. A black key can have two names. If it is between C and D, it can be called C♯ or D♭. The choice of name depends on context. More on this shortly. In modern Western music,

Figure A-4. A two octave range on the keyboard

C♯ and D♭ are considered to be equivalent, in that to the ear they sound exactly the same, and they are referred to as "enharmonic equivalents". Figure A-5 shows the black keys of an octave labeled with both of their enharmonically equivalent letter names.

Since the naming of notes in written music can be ambiguous, and dependent on key signature, as described above, it is useful to adopt a simpler naming convention when one is describing parts of the musical instrument itself, outside the context of musical key. Piano technicians, for instance, always refer to the black keys of the piano as "sharps".

Leaving levers out of the picture for the moment, the harp has seven strings per octave, where the piano has twelve keys. Since the piano can play all twelve notes in the octave, it is referred to as a "chromatic" instrument. The harp, in its original form, had no levers, and played only a diatonic scale, one note per string. For this reason it is known as a diatonic instrument. Modern lever harps give us the ability to change the pitch of the strings by raising or lowering the levers, allowing us to play all the

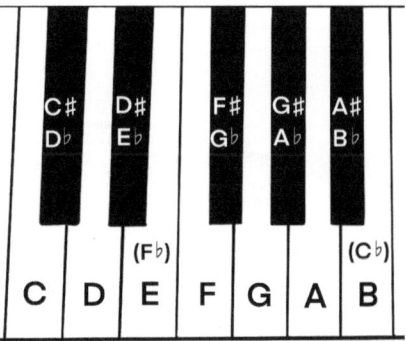

Figure A-5. Black and white keys labeled on a keyboard

notes in the chromatic scale. Nevertheless, because of its historical origins it is still known as a diatonic instrument.

This is a rather esoteric distinction, but it helps us understand that unlike a black piano key that can have more than one letter name, a harp string is always referred to by the same letter name. A C string tuned to C♮, with its lever engaged, plays a C♯, not a D♭. A sharped B♮ string will sound just like C♮ but it is never referred to that way. It is a B♯.

In most music played on the lever harp, while there are technically twelve notes in an octave, only a portion are used in a given piece. Playing this set of notes in a line gives us the scale used in the piece, and the note the scale starts and ends on tells us the key of the piece. Most scales are diatonic, meaning there are seven notes, one for each letter. Depending on the key, a given note might be sharp, flat or natural.

The simplest diatonic scale is the C major scale. This is what you get when you start on any C on a piano and play the white keys up to the next C an octave above. All of the notes are naturals. Major scales have a half step between the third and fourth notes and between the seventh and eighth notes. The rest of the intervals between notes are whole steps. On the piano keyboard, note that there are no black keys between E and F and between B and C. These are the half steps in the C major scale (see Figure A-6). Whether a scale is major or minor (or one of numerous other kinds of scales) depends on where the half steps are found. In any major scale, they are between the third and fourth notes, and between the seventh and eighth notes.

Figure A-6. The C major scale, and the sequence of whole and half steps very different (Figure A-7).

Figure A-7. The natural notes from D to D. Note that half steps have shifted to the left

If one starts playing the white keys on a different note, the resulting scale will not be major because the location of the half steps will be different. Starting a scale on D♮, for instance, places the half steps between the second and third notes and the sixth and seventh notes, resulting in a scale that sounds

However, one can convert any scale into a major scale by altering some of the notes (using the black keys) so that the half step intervals are located correctly. On a D scale, raising the C and the F to sharps (playing C♯ and F♯ instead of the naturals), gives us a D major scale (see Figure A-8).

Since any key but C major will contain at least one sharp or flat note, to avoid writing this symbol every time the note is used, music notation uses a key signature at the very beginning of the piece. The sharped or flatted notes are denoted with symbols on the relevant line or space of the musical staff. A D major key signature has sharp symbols on the C space and the F line (Figure A-9). The symbol to the left of the key signature is called the clef. Clefs tell the musician where a given note will appear on the musical staff. Several different clefs are used in music, but they are not directly relevant to our discussion. In the written examples, we will use the G, or treble clef, the one shown in the illustrations in this appendix.

Looking back to our mention of enharmonic equivalents, a black key on a piano can be referred to by two different names. The one between C and D, for instance, can be either C♯ or D♭. Its name will depend on the key signature. If we are playing in the key of D major, all C notes are sharp. Any C's in the written music will be played on black C♯ key. The white C key will not be used. In the key of D♭ Major, all D notes are flat.

Figure A-8. Making F and C sharp notes gives the whole step – half step sequence of a major scale.

They will be played on the same black key. However, due to the context of our current key, we call the note a D♭. So while on the keyboard, C♯ and D♭ are the same, in written music they are spelled differently, and their naming depends on context.

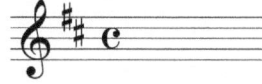

Figure A-9. The key signature of D Major

While we raised two pitches in the sequence of notes from D to D to get a major scale, sometimes it will be necessary to lower pitches to get the correct sequence. In the range of notes from F to F, for instance, the first half step occurs between B and C, which are the fourth and fifth notes in the scale. By lowering B to B flat, we shift the half step to its correct position between the third and fourth notes. The second half step in F major falls naturally in the correct place between E and F, and does not need to be altered.

Now, let's take all this general theory and apply it to the harp. The scale a harp is tuned to is called a tuning. Harps can be tuned to a variety of tunings, but the most common ones are various major keys, including C, F, B♭, and E♭. Refer back to Chapter 2 for illustrations of several of these key signatures. While C major has no flats or sharps, the other three tunings contain various numbers of flats. Tuning in keys containing flats are common because generally a larger number of keys are available to the player (through manipulation of the levers) than keys containing sharps. Since levers can raise pitches and not lower them, tuning harps in "flat" keys allows more choices of different keys to use.

Visually speaking, harps have certain strings color coded to help the harpist find their way. The coding varies among different traditions and cultures, but the most common system is to color the C strings red and the F strings black.

Even the smallest harps have a range of more than one octave, so we also need a system for naming octaves. In the harp world, there is unfortunately more than one way of doing this. The standard used in much of music is the one developed for the keyboard. Since it is frankly a bit more logical than the traditional harp system, let's consider it first.

The piano octave starts on C. The lowest C on a piano is called C1. The C an octave up is C2, and so on. There are a few notes below the lowest C, and these are given zeros, such as A0 and B0.

In the system used in the classical (pedal) harp world, an octave starts on F, and the octave numbers begin at the opposite end of the instrument than the piano. Whereas the lowest full octave on the piano is the first octave, the lowest octave on the harp will have the largest number. A typical 36-string lever harp will often have a 6th octave C as its lowest note. The octave numbers go down as pitches go higher. Figure A-10 shows a section of the harp with strings named by octave and letter.

While piano nomenclature lists the letter before the octave, the reverse is done with harps. We generally write or say "2F" rather than "F2." So 2F is an octave lower than 1F, 3F is lower than 2F, and so on. To make things a bit more confusing, the top F found on modern concert grand harps is not the 1F but 0F. Like the lowest strings on piano, which are below the first octave, the top notes of a concert grand pedal harp are above the first octave. This happened both in harps and pianos because their note range was expanded after the system of numbering the octaves was invented.

These two systems happen to converge in the middle. C4 on the piano and 4C on the pedal harp are both middle C, but it is important to remember the numbers are running in opposite directions.

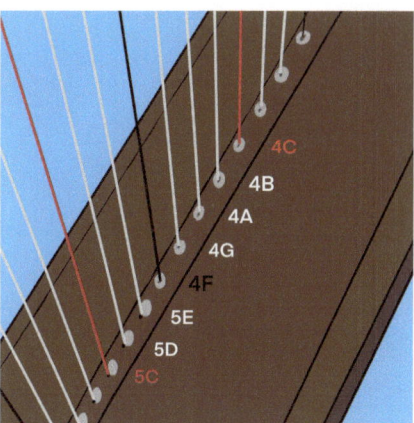

Keep in mind that on many harps, the highest and lowest octaves are often incomplete. Most 34 string harps, for instance, have the first octave A as their top note, so there are only three first octave strings, F, G, and A. This means that the "first" E string on the harp is in the second octave. I've seen countless harps strung

Figure A-10. Strings labeled by octave number and letter

with strings from the wrong octave because of this misunderstanding.

In the lever harp world, some makers simply number the strings from the top starting with one, using whatever letter the harp starts with. No octave numbers are used, simply the number of each string. So a harp might start on a 1A and go down to 34C. If it starts on 1C it might go down to 36C. This system is logical, but not standardized, since any string number can be a different letter depending on the harp. Depending on the number of strings it has, the top string on a given harp using this system could be 1C, 1A, 1G, or some other letter. The number refers to the string's distance form the top of the harp, regardless of letter name.

Some electronic tuners give an octave number when reading a note. This is the piano system, so if you are tuning a harp it is important to be able to translate the number into your harp system. Again, while C4 (piano) and 4C (harp) are the same, C3 and 3C are two octaves apart.

Some lever harp makers use the piano system, others use the pedal harp system, and many more use the system in the preceding paragraph. It is worth checking what system your harp's maker uses. If you are regulating harps for others, make sure you have a common vocabulary when discussing buzzes on a different string.

Of course, many musicians don't know all this terminology, so harpists often refer to notes in relation to middle C. They might say "I think the A an octave above middle C is out of tune when I raise the lever." For this reason it is important to be aware of middle C.

Appendix B: Repairing Stripped Screw Holes

I f you can turn a screw but it never gets tight, the screw hole has most likely become enlarged and is said to be "stripped". If you can't turn a screw because the head has been damaged, we say the screw itself is stripped. Stripped holes are much easier to repair than stripped screws, and we will focus on those here. Stripped screws can sometimes be removed and replaced even if they are too stripped to tighten, but if they can't be removed or are broken off in the wood, seek the help of a professional.

With a stripped hole, there is not enough wood for the screw to bite into, and it doesn't get tight. We have to find a way of making the hole tighter. One option is to use a slightly larger screw, but my first approach is generally to add material to the hole to make it tighter. Since I always have short pieces of thick gut strings to use as anchors, I often use these to tighten stripped holes as well. Cut the piece of gut string short enough to fit in the hole, push it into the screw hole, then insert the screw and tighten. Hopefully it will hold well. You can use more than one piece of gut if needed. The piano technician who taught me this method actually used thin strips of leather, but since I have gut strings readily available I use gut instead. The technician also advised using some wood glue in the hole as well, but I have found that the gut itself does the job quite well. If the hole is too small for a thick piece of gut, you can unwind it and use several individual strands of sinew.

To unwind a strand of gut, you'll need two pairs of pliers. Hold one in each hand and grasp one end of the short strand of gut with each pair of pliers, as shown in Figure B-1. Turn each hand counterclockwise, meaning each hand twists in the opposite direction. This will cause the piece of gut to unwind into separate strands (Figure B-2). When you have a strand of the right thickness, you can cut it to length and insert in the hole, as shown in Figure B-3. You should make it short enough so all of it fits in the hole before you insert the screw. When the strand of gut is inserted, you can replace the screw and tighten it, as shown in Figures B-4 and B-5.

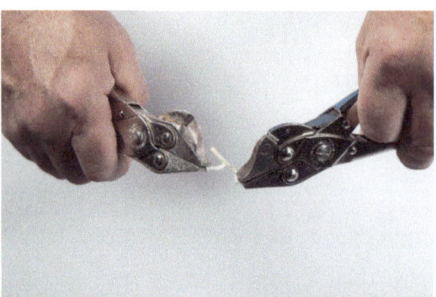

Figure B-1. Create thin strands of gut by unraveling thicker strands.

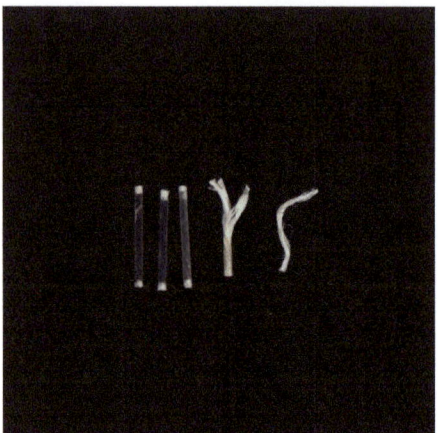

Figure B-2. One inch pieces of thick gut harp strings. Those to the right have been unraveled.

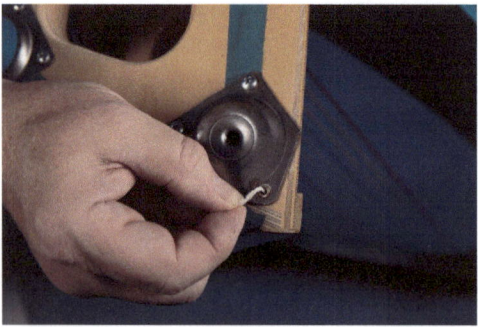

Figure B-3. Insert the strand of gut in the screw hole.

Figure B-4. Replace the screw in the hole

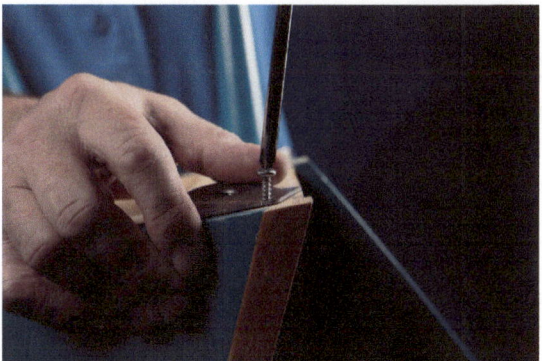

Figure B-5. Drive the screw back in.

If your harp has nylon strings and you don't have a source of used gut strings to use for these repairs, they are available as string ends from companies that sell gut strings.

It is also fairly common to add thin pieces of wood to stripped holes. You can add a small strip of veneer or cut a shaving off a dowel with a sharp utility knife. I generally feel the results are better with gut, but if you have easier access to wood, or you prefer not to use animal products, wood is an option.

If a hole is very badly stripped, you might need to add material AND use a thicker screw. This is fine as long as the larger screw doesn't interfere with whatever you are fastening. The screw holding the lever bracket to the neck, for instance, can only be so large before it will stop fitting through the slot in the bracket. If none of these solutions works, there are others, such as plugging and re-drilling the holes, but they should be left to professionals.

Appendix C: Replacing Levers and Cams

You may need to replace a lever cam if the tip has cracked, or if a note's sound can be improved by using a cam with a smaller groove, as described earlier in this book. You will rarely need to replace the entire lever, unless the bracket has been damaged by an accident or fall.

If you do need to replace a complete lever, loosen the string so that you can move it out of your way. Unscrew the lever from the neck and screw the new one on. Once the new one is installed, you can put the string back in place and tune it up. You will need to regulate the lever using the techniques described elsewhere in this book.

If you are only replacing the cam, it is still best to remove the lever from the harp first. In some cases it is possible to replace the cam with the lever in place, but I don't recommend it, as it is easy to drop the nut on the harp's soundboard and make a dent. In most cases, the levers are too close together to allow enough room for the cam to be removed and a new one installed.

Figure C-1. Removing the lever. Even if you are only replacing a cam, it is best to remove the entire lever.

With the lever off the harp, loosen and remove its nut by turning it counter-clockwise with a 1/4" wrench (Figure C-2). There is a very thin plastic washer between the cam and the nut. Take care not to lose it once you have removed the nut; the cam will not tighten sufficiently without it. If you have ordered a new cam, you will probably receive a new washer as well; if not, you'll want to reuse the old one (see figure C-3).

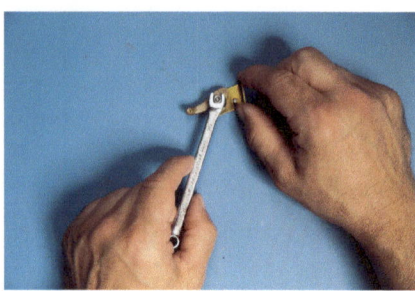

Figure C-2. Remove the cam nut with a 1/4" wrench.

Remove the washer first, or if you have difficulty grasping it, remove the cam while keeping a fingernail on the washer. With the nut and washer out of the way, remove the cam from the rod it is mounted on. Underneath the cam are several additional washers. Leave these alone. There shouldn't be any danger that they will come off while you are switching cams. If any do, they will need to be put back on exactly as they were. Some are spring washers, meaning they need to face a certain direction. If you get into this situation, you should be able to put them back correctly by observing other levers on the harp.

Figure C-3. Make sure there is a washer in place before replacing the nut.

Installing a new cam is simply a matter of performing these steps in reverse. Place the new cam on the rod, followed by the washer, then the nut. If you have a new nut (also probably included with the cam), you should use it as the plastic locking action of these nuts tends to weaken over time.

The final tightening of the cam nut should always happen with the lever on the harp. When you replace the cam nut with the lever removed from the harp the cam will feel deceptively tight. Once you reinstall the lever on the harp you should check and make sure it has the correct tension, enough to keep from buzzing or falling down, but not so tight it stands out from its neighbors. You will also need to check the intonation (see Chapter 7).

Appendix D: The Myth of Perfect Intonation

As I stated in Chapter 7, the goal of regulating a lever is to ensure that when it is engaged, it raises the pitch of the string by exactly one half-step. In practice, this goal is not achievable on every note or every harp. There are a variety of reasons for this, which I'll get into below.

A harp's age can have an effect on intonation. As harps get older, the hundreds or thousands of pounds of tension exerted by the strings cause changes in the harp's wooden structure over time. Soundboards bow upwards. Necks are pulled slightly down. Fore-pillars can bend slightly in the direction of the strings. These distortions can result in changes in relative speaking lengths between the open and sharped pitches on the harp. For a portion of the harp's life, adjusting the levers and bridge pins can compensate for these changes, and this is one reason harps need periodic regulation. Eventually, though, there will come a point where the lever has been adjusted as far as it will go, and the bridge pin driven into the neck as far as possible without buzzing, and the sharped pitch will still be out of tune relative to the open pitch. In some cases, a new hole can be drilled a little higher than the original. Most of the time, though, there is no room for this. Moving the lever up would cause it to hit the bridge pin when engaged. Achieving intonation equal to what the harp was capable of when it was new is impossible without major rebuilding, which would quite possibly be more costly than replacing the harp with a new one.

Another factor is the design decisions that have to be made by harp makers to balance performance quality and price. In a world where cost was no object, in order to achieve the highest possible quality of intonation, ideally each lever would be custom sized to work optimally with the length and diameter of the string it would be fit to. Just as each string is shorter and of lesser diameter than the one before it, each lever would be slightly smaller. In addition, each bridge pin would need to be slightly smaller, allowing the levers to be closer and closer to the string's origin point. While we might not need an individual screw size for each lever, we would probably need at least five or six different sizes of screws, perhaps more.

In the real world, lever harps have much less variation in the sizes of different pieces of hardware. In the case of Loveland levers, there are three bracket and cam sizes, and another fifteen groove sizes. Other brands of levers have a range of anywhere from two to five different sizes. There are generally two to three different sizes of bridge pins on a given harp. In most cases, all the levers are fastened to the neck with the same screws, or maybe there is one larger screw, and one smaller one used in the upper registers. This smaller number of parts does involve some compromise in terms of intonation. This is most notable in the top strings, where it is often hard to get the lever adjusted where it needs to be without running into the bridge pin. The areas of the harp where one size of lever is changed to another can be problematic as well. There are locations on many harps where one size of lever won't allow for perfect regulation, but the next smaller size will be even worse.

If these kinds of intonation problems occur, why don't harp makers use a wider range of lever and pin sizes? Why not make a harp perfect? The answer, of course, is cost. We might think we want perfect intonation, but if harps cost significantly more than they do already, fewer of us could afford them.

The more different parts a harp maker uses on a harp, the more they have to stock, keep track of, and store. They have to drill a wider range of different holes in the necks to accommodate the wider range of different parts, meaning they have to maintain more tools, and the person drilling the holes will have to replace the drill bits in their tools more frequently. In addition, the much smaller parts needed to achieve perfect intonation in the top strings would likely be quite fragile. They would be prone to breakage, especially on student harps played and moved by children. Harp makers would be dealing with more customer complaints and the problem of getting broken parts fixed on a harp that might live thousands of miles from the place where it was manufactured.

These issues may not sound like they would add significantly to a harp's cost, but they would. Every additional bit of complexity in components or manufacturing adds cost. In reality, harp makers need to compete in a marketplace, and this imposes cost constraints.

The good news is that harps can be designed at a reasonable price that can be regulated almost perfectly. They may be perfectly in tune in most strings, but the sharps are just a bit sharper than perfect on the highest strings, and possibly one or two at a break between lever sizes. The imperfections will be slight enough that most people will perceive them as "in tune"; slight enough that the harp can make plenty of beautiful music.

If you regulate your own harp, you may find some strings that you can't regulate perfectly. Do the best with them that you can, and overall the harp should sound good. Know that it is not your fault. You could blame the harp maker, but remember that they did their best to make the best overall product using an imperfect, limited set of lever, string, and bridge pin options.

If you regulate for other people, there will be an occasional harpist who will set up a tuner, show you that your regulation of a particular note is not perfect, and expect you to fix it. In some cases, this will be impossible. This will not be what your customer wants to hear, but it is true. It is simply a fact that not all strings on all harps can be regulated perfectly. If they could be, the harps would be significantly more expensive and less durable.

Acknowledgments

Thank you to Liza Moss for help editing and organizing the manuscript for this book, to Adrienne Maples for most of the photos, and to Marcia Lawrence for copy-editing. Thanks also to Peter Wiley and Norman Friede, for teaching me the basics of lever harp regulation during my earliest days as a technician.

About the Author

Steve Moss has been regulating and repairing harps since 1995. He has serviced instruments throughout North America, for clients including the Milwaukee Symphony, the University of Michigan, the Utah Symphony, the Montreal Symphony, the University of Utah, Brigham Young University, the Eastman School of Music, the Omaha Symphony and the Austin Symphony.

Steve started his harp service career at Lyon & Healy in Chicago, where he oversaw the company's lever harp production before moving into pedal harp assembly and regulation. He also specialized in training new employees and visiting apprentices, and consulted on the development of several new harp models. He has also received training and certification from Camac Harps in France.

Steve holds a Bachelor's Degree in Music Theory and History from Yale University. He has been active as a performing musician and songwriter, both as a solo artist and in groups. He has produced two CDs and plays the guitar, banjo, fiddle, harmonica, and jaw harp.

Steve is the author of *Harp Care with Steve Moss*, the first instructional DVD on harp maintenance, covering tuning, string replacement, cleaning, and moving of pedal and lever harps.